If You Ever Meet a Dinosaur
and Other songs

Music and lyrics by Camilla During
with Wendy Girling-Butcher

Illustrated by Paul Cherrill

BOOSEY & HAWKES
LONDON • NEW YORK • BONN • SYDNEY • TOKYO

2. If you ever meet a dragon climb on its back,
   Climb on its back and give it a pat.
   If you ever meet a dragon climb on its back,
   Do you think you could do that?

3. If you ever meet a monster tell it a joke,
   Tell it a joke and give it a poke.
   If you ever meet a monster tell it a joke.
   Do you think you could do that?

4. If you ever meet a ghost give it a fright,
   Give it a fright and turn on the light.
   If you ever meet a ghost give it a fright
   Do you think you could do that?

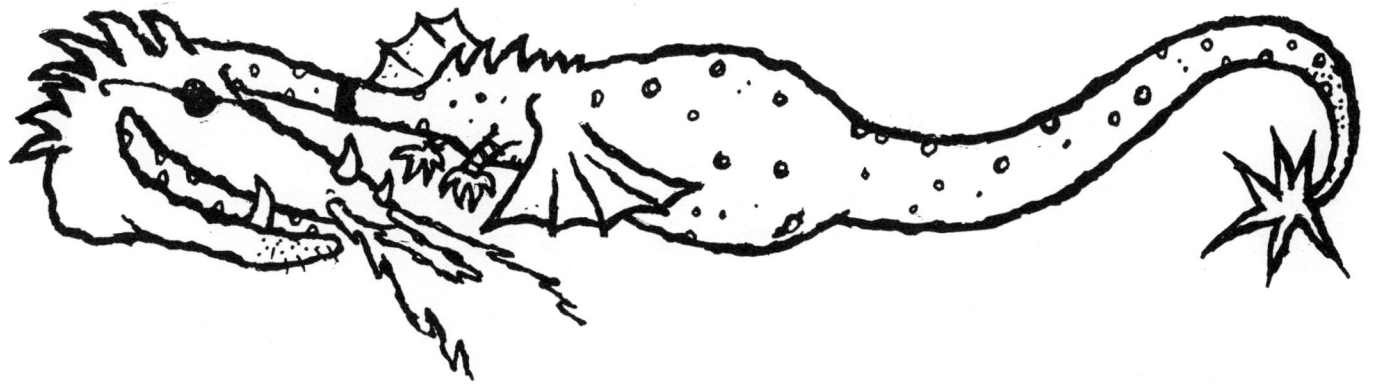

2. Wrinkly Fingers

2. I like to play
   With all my toys.
   I always make
   Lots of noise.
   I splash and splash, *etc.*

3. I love the smell
   Of my shampoo.
   I love the feel
   Of bubbles too.
   I splash and splash, *etc.*

Choose a child to play the mother. The rest of the children are scattered around the room, legs outstretched, pretending to be in the bath. They all do the actions and the mother shouts out her lines.

3. In the Band

2. In the band, in the band,
   There are lots of sounds in the band.
   The woodblock
   Ta ta, *etc.*

3. In the band, in the band,
   There are lots of sounds in the band.
   The jingle bells
   Ta-te ta, *etc.*

4. In the band, in the band,
   There are lots of sounds in the band.
   The tambourine
   Ta-te ta, *etc.*

All the children play their instruments (in time) until a particular one is mentioned. Those with that instrument then have to play their rhythm while the other children listen.
This is a very useful song for children to learn about the different instruments and to listen to others playing. It also requires concentration to play at the correct times.

4. Autumn Leaves

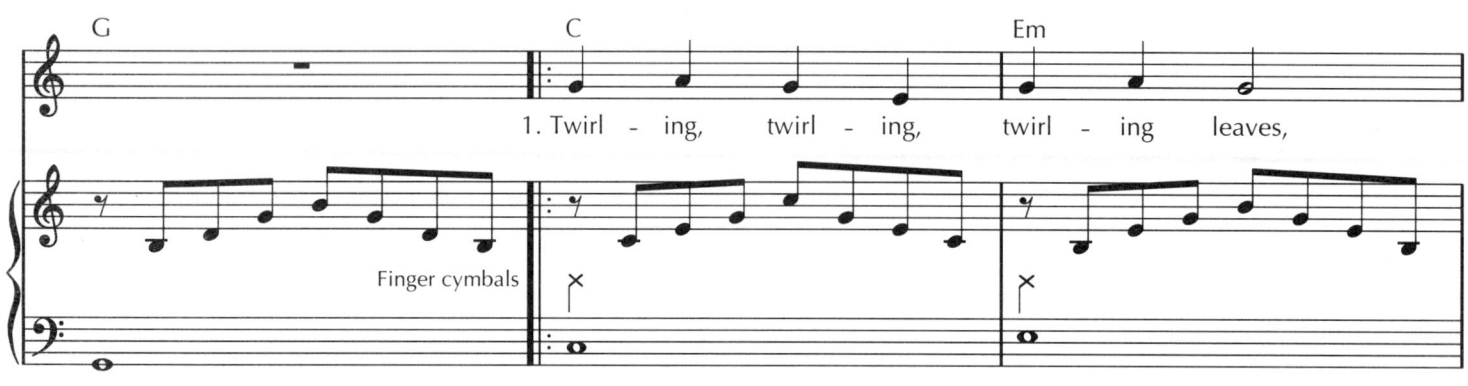
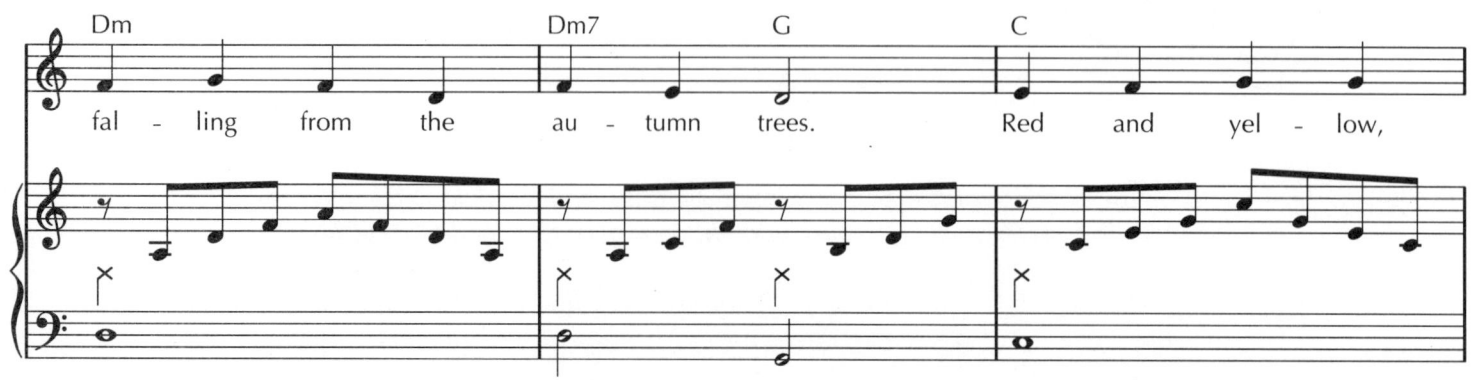

2. Glowing, glowing, glowing trees,
Slowly losing pretty leaves.
See the branches, brown and bare
Nothing left for them to wear.

Children sway and twirl to the music. They particularly enjoy moving with scarves, ribbons or other flowing material. Some children could accompany the music by striking finger cymbals once on the chord changes. Ask them which added instrument is being played in the Interlude. When are two of these instruments playing?

5. You'll Never Guess

*) These words shouted by another group.

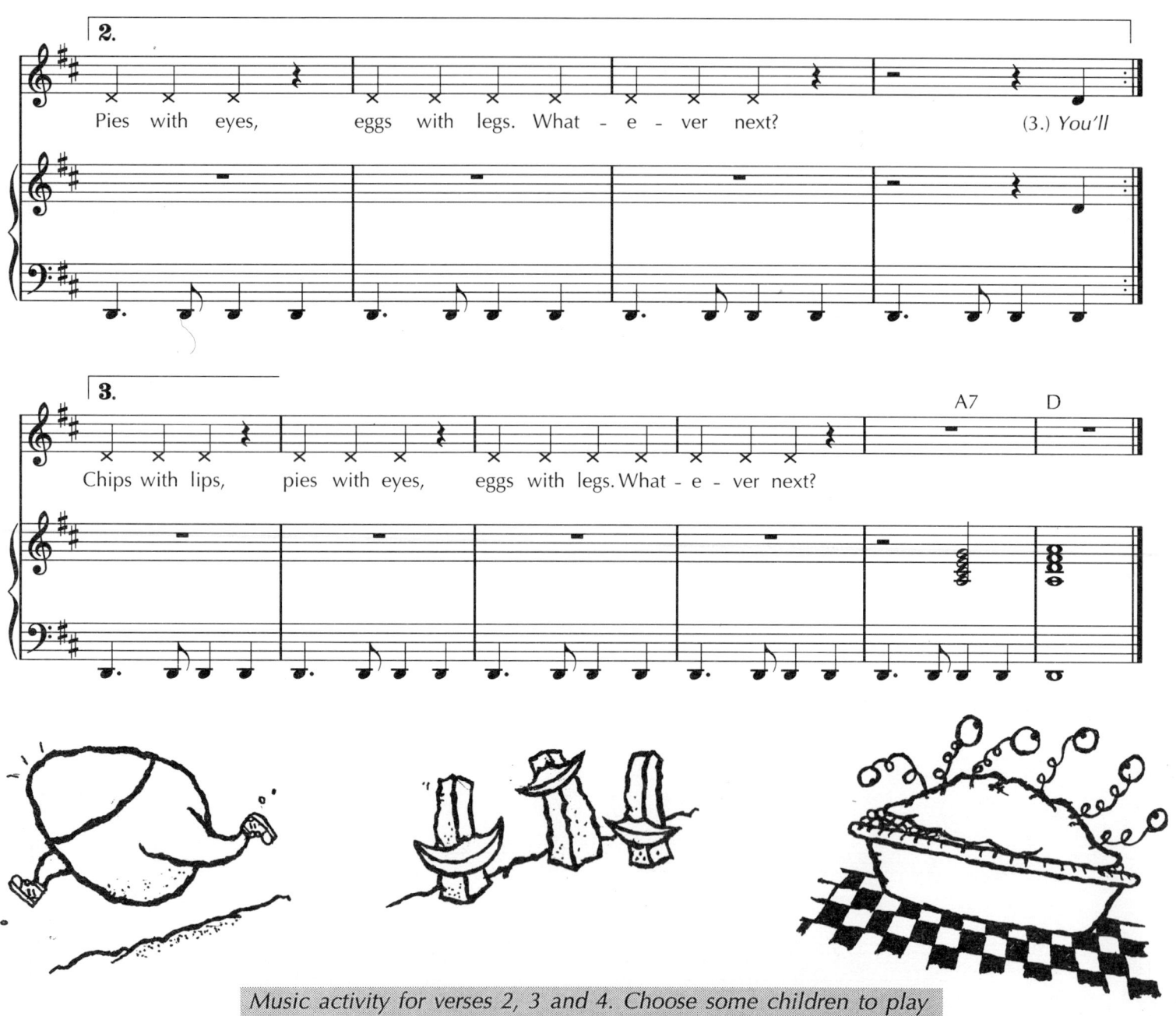

Music activity for verses 2, 3 and 4. Choose some children to play instrumentation as indicated in the music. You will need finger cymbals and/or triangles, and woodblocks. Children who aren't playing instruments can move like trees and sway in time to the music.

6. In My Garden

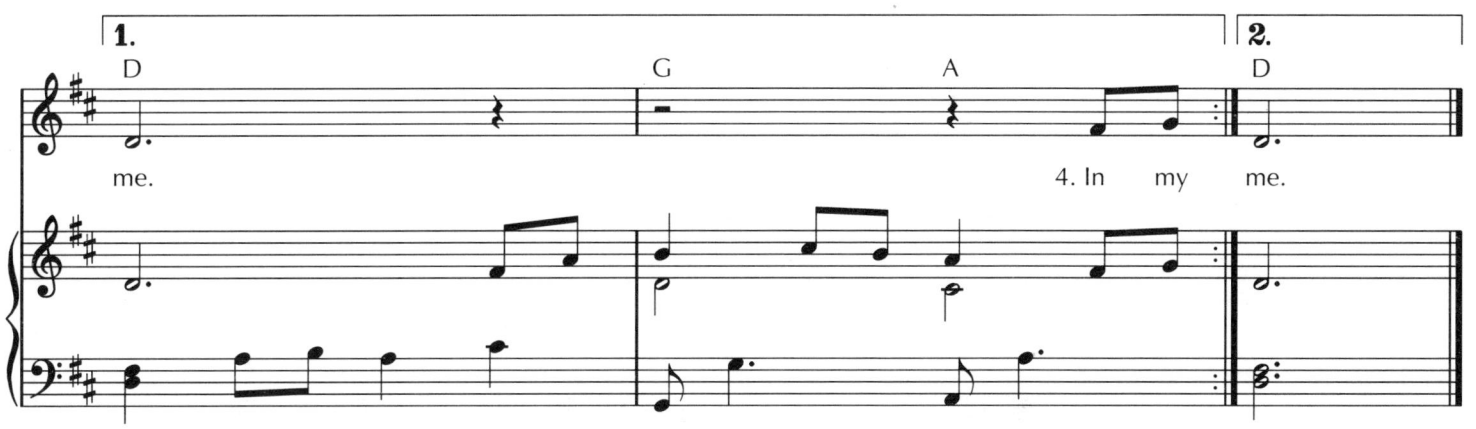

Some of the children can sing the song and some can shout out the repeated words. Children enjoy illustrating this song.

7. Clap, Clap

Perform body percussion as indicated in the music.
Children can play percussion instruments as in the musical interlude on the tape. Have four groups — small woodblocks for the "claps"; two tone woodblocks for the "pats"; drums for the "stamps" and finger cymbals for the "clicks".

8. The Insect Dance

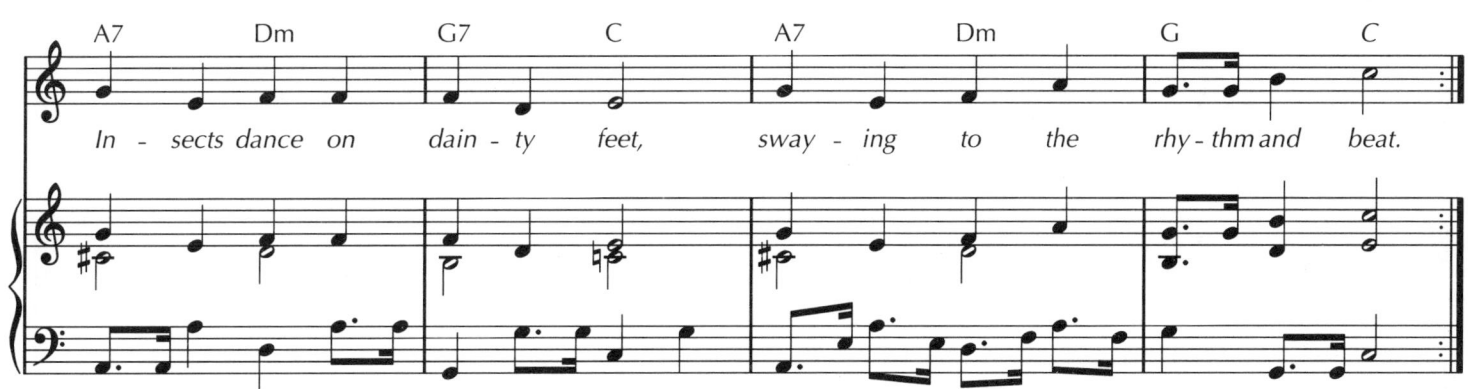

2. Can you see them all have fun?
   See the ants, they run, run, run.
   Bees hurry scurry out of their hive.
   Busy wee fellows twist and jive.
   Chorus

3. Come along and have a fling.
   Hear cicadas sing, sing, sing.
   See the little beetles scuttle and skip.
   Dragonflies quiver and flit, flit, flit.
   Chorus

Children can perform a circle dance. Dance steps can be created from the words of the song using the children's ideas.

9. Who's That?

hands. It's Sa-rah, Sa-rah, clap, clap, clap-ping her hands.

2. Who's that in the middle of the circle
Dance, dance, dancing around?
It's Daniel, Daniel,
Dance, dance, dancing around.

3. Who's that in the middle of the circle
Nod, nod, nodding her head?
It's Zoe, Zoe,
Nod, nod, nodding her head.

4. Who's that in the middle of the circle
Stamp, stamp, stamping his feet?
It's David, David,
Stamp, stamp, stamping his feet.

New verses can be made up. Choose a child to go into the middle of the circle. He/she invents an action – pat knees, jump, twirl, etc. The other children sing the song modifying the words where necessary. This movement song is very popular with children as they all love to have centre stage!

11. Rosie

*) A separate group can sing these echoes.

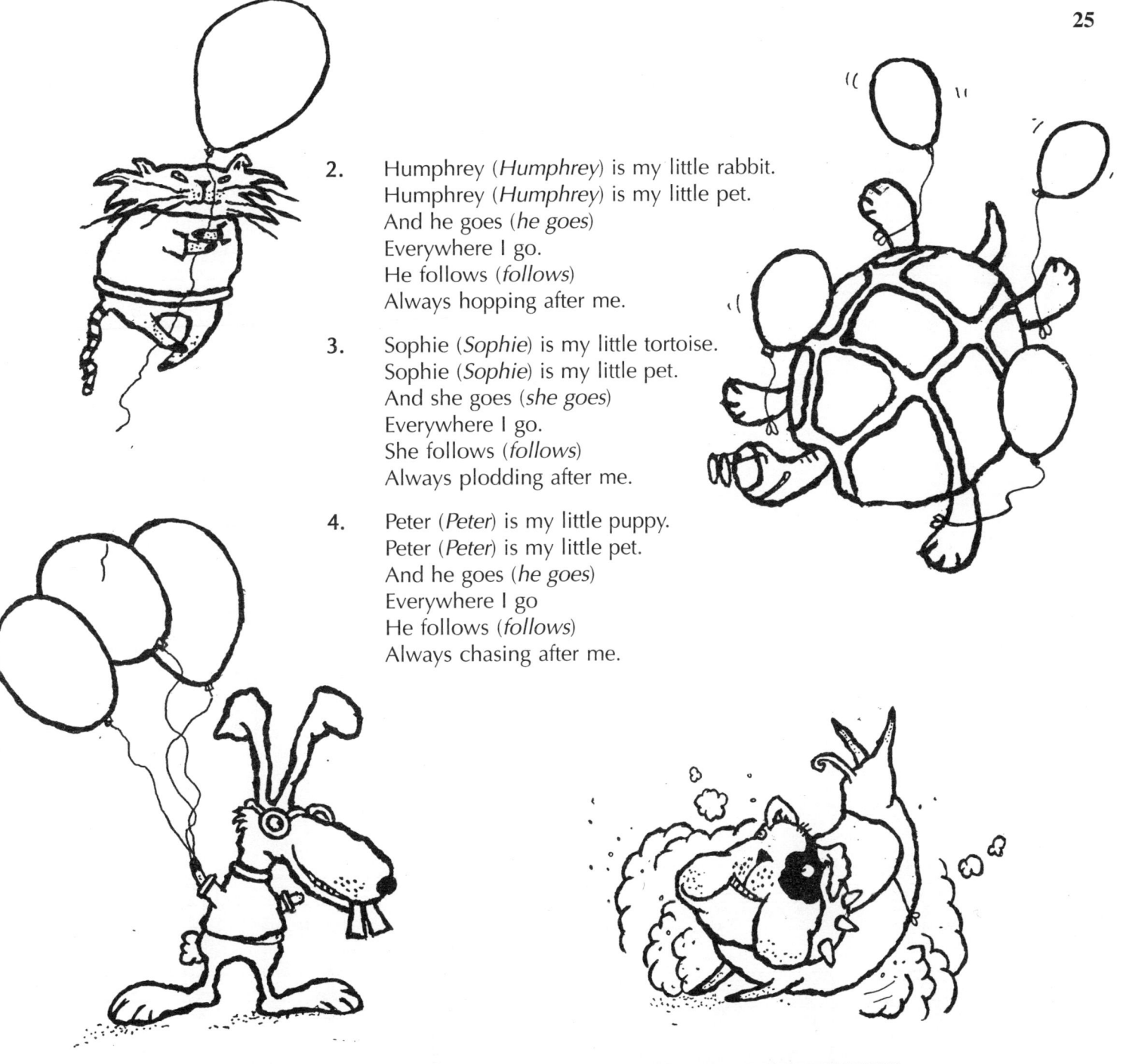

2. Humphrey (*Humphrey*) is my little rabbit.
   Humphrey (*Humphrey*) is my little pet.
   And he goes (*he goes*)
   Everywhere I go.
   He follows (*follows*)
   Always hopping after me.

3. Sophie (*Sophie*) is my little tortoise.
   Sophie (*Sophie*) is my little pet.
   And she goes (*she goes*)
   Everywhere I go.
   She follows (*follows*)
   Always plodding after me.

4. Peter (*Peter*) is my little puppy.
   Peter (*Peter*) is my little pet.
   And he goes (*he goes*)
   Everywhere I go
   He follows (*follows*)
   Always chasing after me.

Choose a group of children to sing the echoes throughout the song. Children can create their own verses using their pets' names.

12. Get Out!

2. There are pigs wearing wigs in the garden.
   There are pigs wearing wigs outside.
   Chorus
   Shall we stamp and shout and tell them to get out?
   Boo! (*Boo!*) Shoo! (*Shoo!*) Get out!

3. There's a cow going miaow in the garden.
   There's a cow going miaow outside.
   Chorus
   Shall we stamp and shout and tell her to get out?
   Boo! (*Boo!*) Shoo! (*Shoo!*) Get out!

4. There's a lion and he's crying in the garden.
   There's a lion and he's crying outside.
   Chorus
   Shall we stamp and shout and tell him to get out?
   No! *No!* No! Give him a hug.

Choose a group of children to shout out the repeated words in each verse. This song can be very successfully dramatised and it also makes a terrific wall story.

13. We Can Hear You

2. We can hear you playing on the cymbals.
   Ta ta ta ta playing on the cymbals.
   We can hear you playing on the cymbals.
   Ta ta ta ta ta sa sa sa.

3. We can hear you playing the maracas, *etc.*

4. We can hear you playing all together, *etc.*

5. We can hear you playing very softly, *etc.*

Divide the children into instrumental groups. Each group plays its instruments as indicated in the song. Encourage them to play on the beat – e.g.
/ / / / / / / /
We can hear you playing on the woodblock.
Practise the last line with the children by first clapping it while counting out loud – e.g. 1, 2, 3, 4, 5, sa, sa, sa. ("Sa, sa, sa," should be whispered.)

14. Let's Make Noises

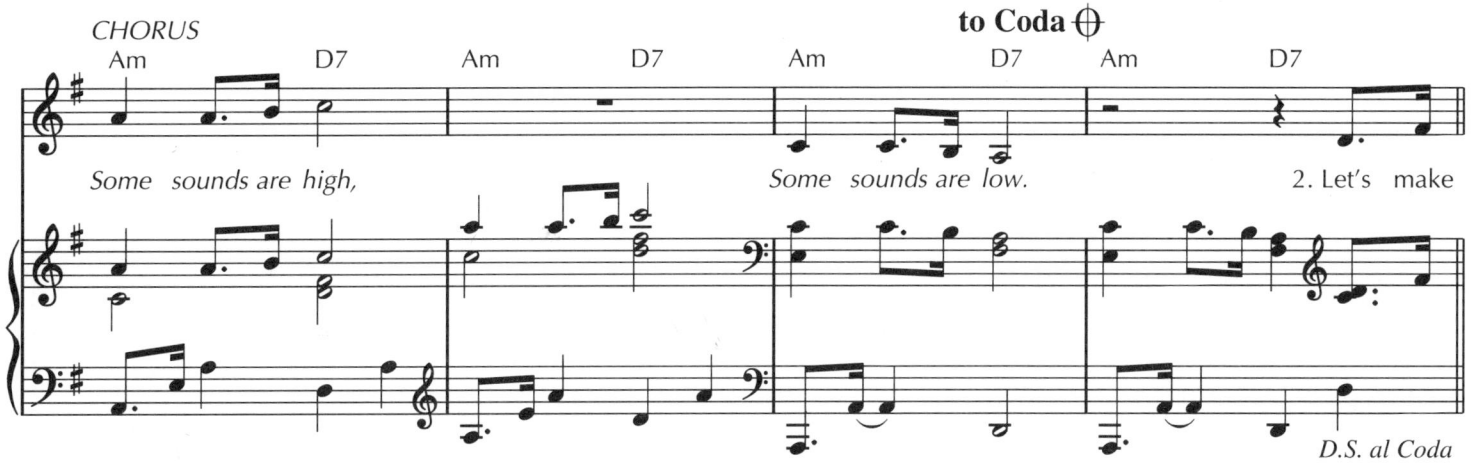

2. Let's make noises like a chick.
   Cheep, cheep, cheep, cheep.
   Let's make noises like a dog.
   Woof, woof, woof, woof.

   Let's make noises like a cat.
   Miaow, miaow, miaow, miaow.
   Let's make noises like a cow.
   Moo, moo, moo, moo.

   Chorus

To encourage the children to use their head voice, ask them to squeak very high at the appropriate places. This helps with their pitching. They can raise their arms for the high sounds and touch the ground for the low sounds.

15. My Place

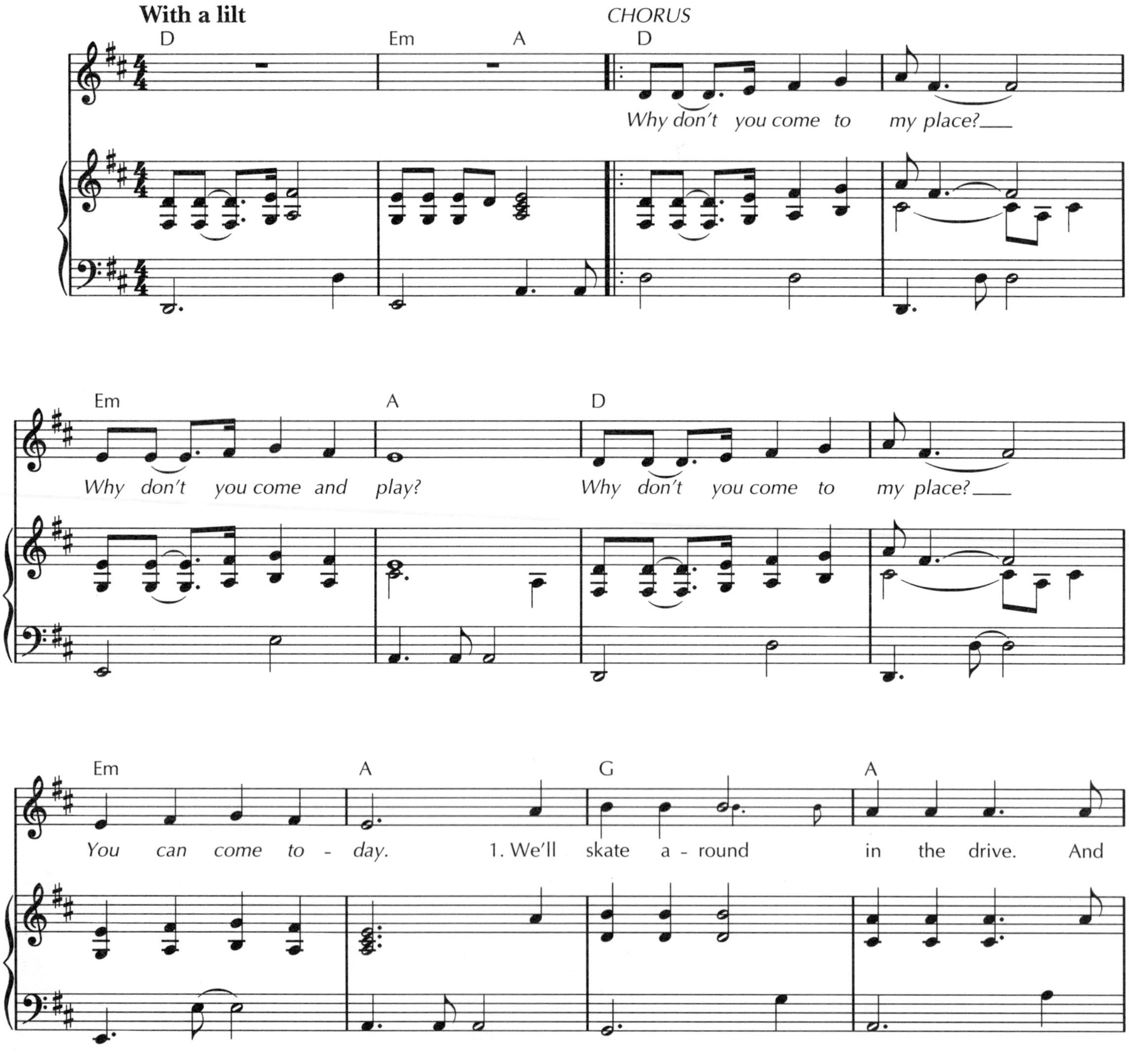
With a lilt
CHORUS
D
Em
A
D
Why don't you come to my place?
Em
A
D
Why don't you come and play?
Why don't you come to my place?
Em
A
G
A
You can come to - day.
1. We'll skate a - round in the drive. And

Chorus

2. We'll build a house up in my tree
   And take a yummy picnic tea.
   I really hope that you can come
   'Cos we'll have such fantastic fun.

Chorus

3. We'll play some games and I'll be kind.
   I'll even let you win sometimes.
   I really hope that you can come
   So hurry up and ask your mum.

16. Can You Eat Your Teddy Bear?

2. Can you eat a bumble bee?
Can I eat a bumble bee?
Can you nibble your knee?
Can I nibble my knee?
Can you chew your mum's shoe?
Can I chew my mum's shoe?
Or the sticky old glue?
Or the sticky old glue?

The teacher or able child/children can sing the initial questions and the rest of the class can sing the responding questions. Everyone can join in for the chorus. Children may like to compose their own "silly" questions.

17. You Can Jump

Change the accompaniment for every verse if possible, e.g.

2. You can dance when hear the dancing music, *etc.*
3. You can march when you hear the marching music, *etc.*
4. You can run when you hear the running music, *etc.*
5. You can hop when you hear the hopping music, *etc.*
6. You can skip when you hear the skipping music, *etc.*

The teacher or able children can accompany some of the verses of the song with a drum or tambourine as follows:

March – use quarter beats (crotchets) – ta ta ta ta, etc.
Jump – use quarter notes with quarter beat – ta sa ta sa, etc.
Skip – use dotted rhythm – ta-ti ta-ti ta-ti ta-ti, etc.

18. What Can You Do?

2. What can you do? What can you do?
   We can make our bed and shut the door.
   We can clean the bath and sweep the floor.
   We can wriggle our hips and count to ten.
   We can brush out teeth and write with a pen.

3. What can you do? What can you do?
   We can write our name and feed the cat.
   We can hop and skip. Can you do that?
   We can whistle a tune and sing a song.
   We can clap the beat as we sing along.

Divide the class in half. One half sings one line and the other half sings the next line and so on throughout the song. Children may like to make up their own answers.

19. Jake

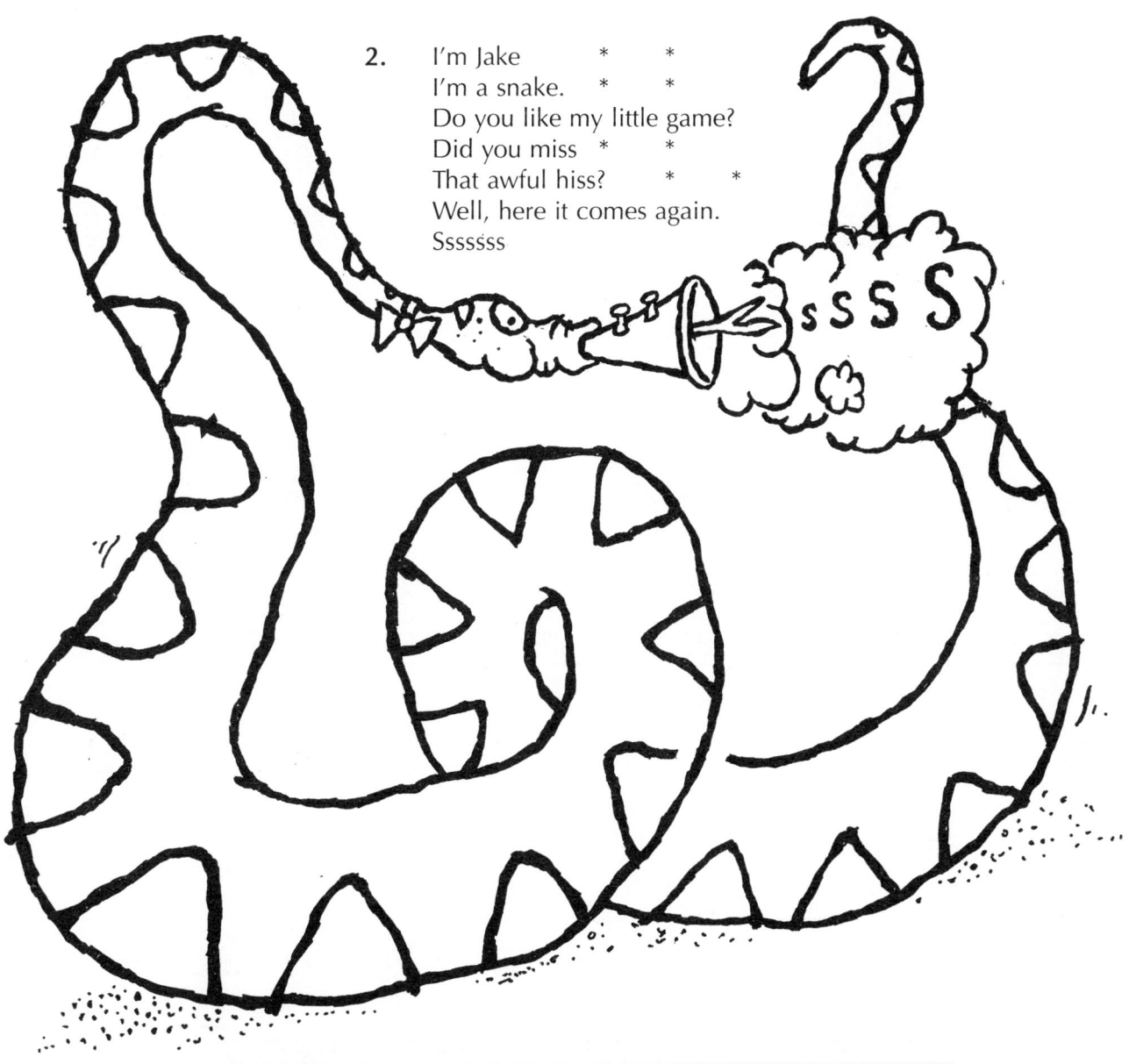

2. I'm Jake   *   *
I'm a snake.   *   *
Do you like my little game?
Did you miss   *   *
That awful hiss?   *   *
Well, here it comes again.
Sssssss

Children can tap – one index finger on top of the other – as indicated in the music and lyrics. For the line, 'Do you like my little game?' they can make snake movements with their arms. They can also make hand puppets out of socks, or finger puppets, and dramatise the song.

20. Summer Lullaby

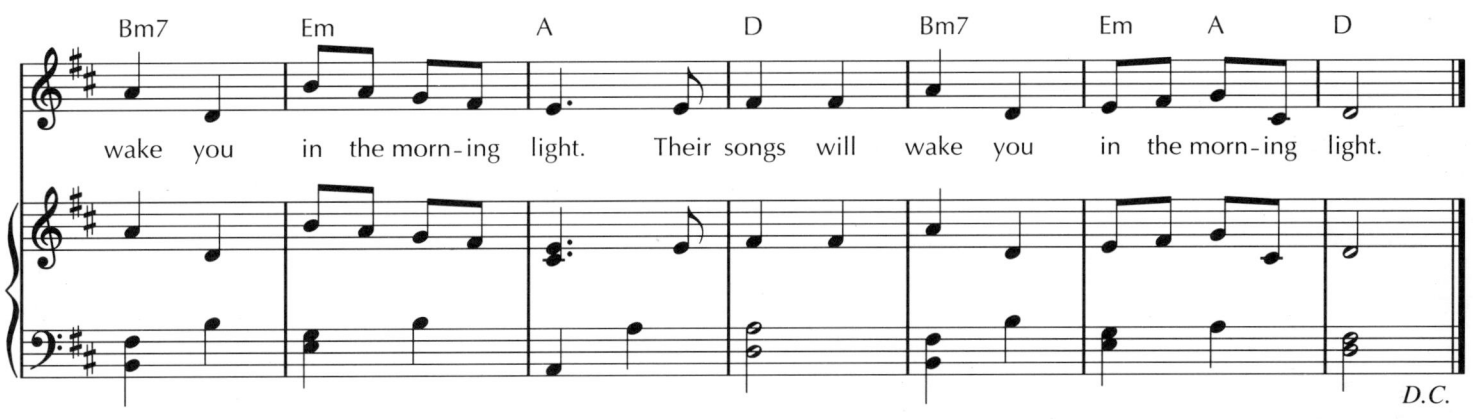

2. Listen to the leaves outside your window.
Listen to the breeze whisper and sigh.
Softly sleep on your pillow, little heart.
The sky is alight with the twinkling stars.
All your sleepy friends are resting for the night.
They will call you in the morning light.
They will call you in the morning light.

Children can have a quiet time while they listen to this song. Ask them if they know what the added instrument is and what the bird call is at the end. (It is a New Zealand owl called the ruru.)

Contents

1. If You Ever Meet a Dinosaur — 2
2. Wrinkly Fingers — 4
3. In the Band — 6
4. Autumn Leaves — 8
5. You'll Never Guess — 10
6. In My Garden — 13
7. Clap, Clap — 16
8. The Insect Dance — 18
9. Who's That? — 20
10. Flying — 22
11. Rosie — 24
12. Get Out! — 26
13. We Can Hear You — 28
14. Let's Make Noises — 30
15. My Place — 32
16. Can You Eat Your Teddy Bear — 34
17. You Can Jump — 36
18. What Can You Do? — 38
19. Jake — 40
20. Summer Lullaby — 42

Music set by Andrew Jones
Cover layout by Sue Clarke

IMPORTANT NOTICE: The unauthorised copying of the whole or any part of this publication is illegal